Wisdom for the BusyCoach

VOLUME TWO

By Stephanie Zonars

CROSSTRAINING
PUBLISHING

Wisdom for the BusyCoach - Volume Two
Copyright © 2016 by Stephanie Zonars
Published by Cross Training Publishing

CROSS TRAINING PUBLISHING
Cross Training Publishing, LLC Omaha Nebraska
gordon@crosstrainingpublishing.com
crosstrainingpublishing.com

Press inquiries: gordon@crosstrainingpublishing.com

cover art provided by: istockphoto.com
author photo by: Mark Selders

Printed in the United States of America
First Printing: March 2016

ISBN   978-1-938254-50-5

With a humble and grateful heart
I dedicate this book to Jesus Christ,
the source of all wisdom.

leadership

You have to learn how
to get comfortable with
being uncomfortable.
—Lou Pinella

Leadership is uncomfortable, **BusyCoach**. Whether it's public speaking, confronting poor performance or firing an employee, every leader has responsibilities that make him squirm. Growing in leadership means growing comfortable with discomfort.

The alternative—firmly planting one's feet in the comfort zone—feels safe, but may result in complacency, stagnancy and even boredom. A comfortable leader feels in control, but can easily get stuck in a rut from being under-challenged.

Leaders who are growing embrace discomfort because they know that stretching leads to greater strength. The challenge to develop or refine skills keeps leaders sharp and engaged, warding off the dullness that comes with the status quo.

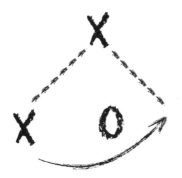

How will you get more comfortable with the uncomfortable today?

By faith Abraham, when called to go to a place he would later receive as his inheritance, obeyed and went, even though he did not know where he was going.

—*Hebrews 11:8 (NIV)*

champion

You don't have to win a
championship to be a champion.
—Don Meyer

Most **BusyCoach**es define a champion as the individual or team that comes in first place. Yet only a few teams finish the season with a win. In fact, many compete for years and never win a championship.

The dictionary defines a champion as a fighter or warrior. Champions keep fighting no matter what the scoreboard says. Champions battle through all the uncontrollables of competition (and life) by focusing on what they can control. Champions fight for a higher value or purpose. Champions never, ever give up.

All competitors strive for championships, and many become discouraged when they don't achieve that goal.

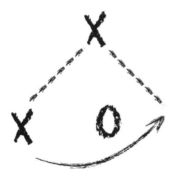

Remember, hoisting a championship trophy isn't the only way to become a champion.

But as for you, be strong and courageous, for your work will be rewarded.

—2 Chronicles 15:7

action

You never plow a field by
turning it over in your mind.

—Irish Proverb

Your mind, **BusyCoach**, is chock-full of ideas, scenarios and challenges. They start churning as soon as your feet hit the floor each morning, and you're hard-pressed to turn them off each night. So many thoughts, so little time!

Effective leaders balance mulling over the issues of the day and making decisive calls. The job won't get done unless you take action. Yet it's easy to get paralyzed by the desire for more information or clarity.

Mature leaders become comfortable making the best decision possible with the information and clarity they have in the moment. The more they practice, the easier it gets.

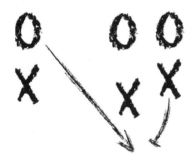 What decision requires your action today?

Therefore, get your minds ready for action, being self-disciplined, and set your hope completely on the grace to be brought to you at the revelation of Jesus Christ.

—*1 Peter 1:13*

gratitude

If you see no reason for giving thanks, the fault lies within yourself.

—Tecumseh

Each day, **BusyCoach**, thousands of messages bombard you. Some from the Internet or TV. Others from small talk about the coach at another school with a bigger budget, better gear and more gadgets. All of them try to get you to want more.

They heighten your awareness of what you don't have and supposedly need. This leads to comparisons that bring discontent, anxiety and a hunger for more. Truth is, most of us enjoy more clothes, food and toys than we need to survive.

Focusing on what you *do* have brings peace. Living each day with a spirit of thankfulness for your blessings keeps you grounded and mindful that more stuff won't bring you more meaning and purpose.

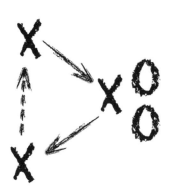

Whatever life brings your way this week, take the opportunity to express thanks.

Give thanks to the Lord and proclaim his greatness. Let the whole world know what he has done.

—1 Chronicles 16:8

courage

It is curious that physical courage should be so common in the world and moral courage so rare.

—Mark Twain

You strive to live courageously, **BusyCoach**. To compete without fear of opponents, mistakes or all-in commitment. You model this kind of courage for your players by confidently facing tough situations or willingly taking risks.

But there's another kind of courage—moral courage. It refuses to remain silent when faced with injustice or cheat the system when presented an opportunity.

Standing up for what's morally right may cost you relationships or even your job. But failing to show moral courage costs much, much more. Shattered lives. Ruined integrity. Destroyed trust.

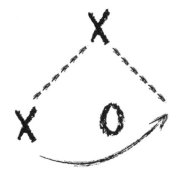

Where will you show moral courage today?

So be strong and courageous, all you who put your hope in the Lord!

—*Psalm 31:24*

margin

 I think God's going to come
down and pull civilization over
for speeding.

—Steven Wright

For many **BusyCoach**es, break-neck speed is the new normal. All-year-round traveling, recruiting and practicing, not to mention the demands of managing a dynamic team of people. Rushing through life is commonplace.

It doesn't have to be this way. You can create margin for rest and recovery and still be a winning coach. I know a highly successful Power 5 Conference coach who takes off a full 24 hours from work each week (and gives her staff the same— even during the season). All while maintaining a top-ranked program.

Don't get a ticket for speeding through life. Slow down. Smell roses. Enjoy people. Make memories.

Be still and know that I am God!

—Psalm 46:10

example

 People are changed, not by coercion or intimidation, but by example.

—John Maxwell

BusyCoaches use all sorts of approaches in helping players grow and change. Some demean and downgrade (maybe if people feel less than human they will change?). Others yell and scream (maybe if people feel intimidated they will change?). But neither results in long-term change.

You'll get further, faster, by modeling what you want them to grasp. Want a player to become more responsible? Show her what it looks like to keep a commitment even though you don't want to. Want an assistant to get that scout to you on time? Show her how to meet deadlines by meeting your own. Want your players to treat people with respect? Show them how by respecting janitors, equipment room managers and ushers.

People will temporarily change under duress, just to survive. But if you want to promote lasting change in your program, you've got to lead the way by example.

What example will you set today?

[Jesus speaking] I have given you an example to follow.

—John 13:15

productivity

 It takes less time to do the
right thing than to explain
why you did it wrong.
—Henry Wadsworth Longfellow

Every **BusyCoach** is on the lookout for the latest time-saving methods to increase productivity and efficiency. All the latest tech advances are efforts to multiply time.

Yet one of the easiest roads to efficiency is simply doing the right thing. Sports pages everywhere detail how coaches waste time when they don't do the right thing. Hundreds if not thousands of hours spent in meetings, press conferences and NCAA investigations to explain and address errors in judgment or outright cheating.

BusyCoaches who do the right thing stay on track to reach team goals. They get there faster by avoiding the circle-back explanations and emergency meetings that result from doing the wrong thing.

If you're looking to become more efficient, consider the impact of simply doing what's right.

The LORD will withhold no good thing from those who do what is right.

—Psalm 84:11b

failure

 Failure is an event,
not a person.

—Jim Tressel

Failure happens, **BusyCoach**. Sometimes we lose. Sometimes we make mistakes. Sometimes we get fired. Not one person on Earth is free from failure. In fact, some of history's most successful people experienced many failures.

One difference between good leaders and great ones lies in how they handle failure. Great leaders refuse to be defined by it, viewing it as an event rather than their identity. They take learning points from it and figure out how to keep moving forward.

Learning how to rebound from failure is one of life's most important skills, both for you and your team. This generation of athletes doesn't fail well. Take every opportunity to teach your team how to resist internalizing failure and use it as an important lesson to help them reach their potential.

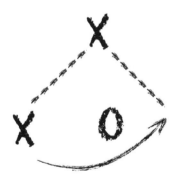

How are you training your players to handle failure?

My health may fail, and my spirit may grow weak, but God remains the strength of my heart; he is mine forever.

—*Psalm 73:26*

fear

 We must build dikes of courage
to hold back the flood of fear.
—Martin Luther King, Jr.

Every **BusyCoach** deals with fear of some shape or form. As youngsters, we fear the dark, the high dive or spiders. As adults, our fears become more sophisticated like losing a job, public speaking or making the wrong decision.

Fear lurks around the corners of our lives, holding us back from being all we are created to be. It exists, it's real and it's probably not going away. So it's crucial to learn how to manage our fears and move forward in spite of them, rather than trying to eliminate the inevitable.

Most often that means doing the very things we fear. Though we may not intentionally lose our job, anyone who gets fired finds out it's typically not the end of the world. Face the fear of speaking in public and slowly it loses its grip. Make the best decisions possible with the information in hand and realize that most of them work out OK.

What fear will you face to build a "dike of courage?"

But immediately Jesus said to them: "Take courage! It is I. Don't be afraid."

—Matthew 14:27 (NIV)

risk

 Behold the turtle. He makes
progress only when he sticks
his neck out.
—James Bryant Conant

Sometimes, **BusyCoach**, it's easier to play it safe. Maintain the status quo. Refuse to rock the boat. Like a turtle that feels threatened, you may pull yourself in under that hard, protective shell and hide.

But moving forward in leadership means stepping out of your comfort zone and taking risks. Voice an opposing opinion to your head coach. Let your assistant make in-game substitutions. Stand up for yourself when you feel intimidated.

Growth requires getting comfortable with being uncomfortable. Sticking your neck out may leave you feeling vulnerable in the short-term, but you'll go further in the long run.

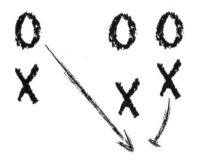

What risk will you take today?

As Jesus was walking along, he saw a man named Matthew sitting at his tax collector's booth. "Follow me and be my disciple," Jesus said to him. So Matthew got up and followed him.

—Matthew 9:9

leadership

 I start with the premise that the function of leadership is to produce more leaders, not more followers.

—Ralph Nader

*BusyCoach*es love the satisfaction found in helping young people develop into positive, contributing members of society. All the blood, sweat and tears invested isn't just to win games. They also ensure that athletes leave the program better leaders than when they entered it.

Looking through this lens, leadership means influence, not authority. Less iron fist and more shepherding.

Coaches often trace the issues on their teams back to a lack of leadership and yet fail to teach their players how to lead. Although some players may possess natural skills, many aspects of leadership must be taught.

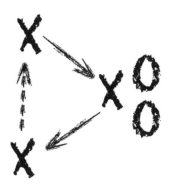

Take time to explain the skills required and offer opportunities to practice them.

But commission Joshua, and encourage and strengthen him, for he will lead this people across and will cause them to inherit the land that you will see.

—*Deuteronomy 3:28*

change

 Your life does not get
better by chance, it gets
better by change.

—Jim Rohn

BusyCoaches relentlessly seek new strategies to give them that needed edge. However, while the pursuit of team goals takes center stage, life goals are oftentimes left to chance.

When you think of who you want to be in 5 or 10 years—not only in your career, but as a person—what do you see? Just like with your team, you'll never get there by leaving it to chance. Realizing that vision will take proactive, intentional change. Little adjustments that will make a big difference in the end.

What areas need your attention today? Relationships? Finances? Health? Faith? Career? Clarify the destination, assess where you are right now and make some changes to help you get there!

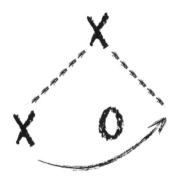

What small change will you make today?

And he [Jesus] said: "Truly I tell you, unless you change and become like little children, you will never enter the kingdom of heaven."

—Matthew 18:3 (NIV)

health

 Health is like money, we never have a true idea of its value until we lose it.

—Josh Billings

Although most **BusyCoach**es once competed athletically, some forsake regular exercise now. It's easy to take good health for granted until a test result or diagnosis turns our world upside down. Sometimes by then, it's too late to get it back.

Caring for our bodies in no way guarantees that we will prevent disease or live longer. Yet the benefits of exercise overwhelmingly increase our likelihood of good health and wellness. You know this. But something (work, family, TV, life) impedes you from pursuing fitness. What's in your way?

What small changes can you implement to take care of your body? A daily walk at lunch? Healthy snacks in your desk drawer? Water instead of soda? Even little changes can make a huge difference in your energy level and ability to focus.

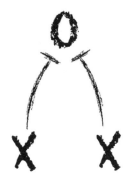

What's your strategy for better health?

Dear friend, I hope all is well with you and that you are as healthy in body as you are strong in spirit.

—3 John 1:2

process

 There are no shortcuts to
anyplace worth going.
—Beverly Sills

We live in the era of the quick-fix, **BusyCoach**. Attention spans shrink daily in our instant culture of tickers, texts and Twitter. So what naturally happens when we have goals? We want to get there now!

The best part of reaching a destination or a goal isn't the arrival itself but the journey. Beauty lies in the adversity we overcome, the people we meet and the joy we experience along the way. Shortcuts usually only result in backtracks later to correct mistakes.

So wherever you're headed, don't resist the long way. Cherish the joys and the bumps in the road—they will make your arrival all the more meaningful!

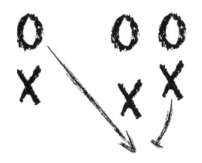

What part of the process will you focus on today?

When Pharaoh finally let the people go, God did not lead them along the main road that runs through Philistine territory, even though that was the shortest route to the Promised Land.

    —Exodus 13:17

perspective

 Enjoy the little things, for one
day you may look back and
realize they were the big things.
—Robert Brault

Some **BusyCoach**es obsess over "little things." Touching the line in a conditioning drill. Eye contact. Shirts tucked in. Why? Because those little things make big things—your culture, your season, your success.

It's true in life, too. Focus only on achievement, and you'll overlook little things.

Calling a colleague just to say hi. Drinking in the beauty of a flower. Kissing your child's boo-boo. Your life's tapestry is woven from millions of moments just like these, not earth-shattering events.

Whether you do them and *how* you do them matters. Race through life, and you'll miss the joy the little things bring.

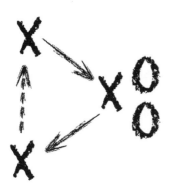

And in the end, you'll realize they weren't so little after all.

The heavens proclaim the glory of God. The skies display his craftsmanship.

—*Psalm 19:1*

leadership

 As we look ahead into the next century, leaders will be those who empower others.

—Bill Gates

Leadership styles come in a variety of shapes and sizes, **BusyCoach**. Maybe you've heard them described, for example, as transactional, autocratic, democratic, charismatic, participative or transformative. Truth be told, any of these styles work. The one to use depends on the situation at hand.

No matter their leadership style, the best leaders empower others. They are for their people. Followers feel championed and supported rather than discouraged or opposed. These leaders want their people to soar!

Joe Ehrmann, author of *InSideOut Coaching*, asks it this way: "What does it feel like to be coached by you?"

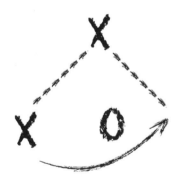

Do your players feel empowered or overpowered?

But you will receive power when the Holy Spirit comes upon you. And you will be my witnesses, telling people about me everywhere—in Jerusalem, throughout Judea, in Samaria, and to the ends of the earth.

—Acts 1:8

friendship

The better part of one's
life consists of his friendships.
—Abraham Lincoln

Ask a **BusyCoach** how things are going, and 9 out of 10 times the answer is "busy!" In season or out, life is full. Coaching is not a 9 to 5 gig, and many coaches feel the responsibility or pressure (or both) to be available to players (and even recruits) 24/7.

Something has to give, and it's usually your personal life. Relationships with family and friends take a hit, especially during the season.

Yet staying meaningfully connected to the most important people in your life proves crucial to sustaining perspective, sanity and balance. These folks remind you of the bigger picture—there's more to life than your sport, team or season.

Your relationships comprise the best part of your life!

They will keep growing despite your busyness if you create habits to nurture them.

A friend is always loyal, and a brother is born to help in time of need.

—Proverbs 17:17

heart

 Heart is what separates the good from the great.

—Michael Jordan

You're on the lookout for an edge, **BusyCoach**. That special ingredient to elevate your team to the championship level. One of the biggest difference-makers, however, won't be found in the realm of new conditioning drills, offenses or strategies.

Many teams have talented coaches and players. But not every team boasts individuals with heart—people motivated by an irrepressible want to, and distinguished by their work ethic and never give up attitudes. One player with heart makes all the difference!

You can't coach heart, so you've got to find athletes who already possess it. The spark he or she brings will inspire your team toward greater success!

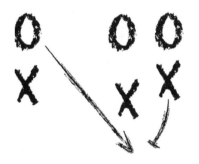

Which players on your team have heart?

Whatever you do, work at it with all your heart, as working for the Lord, not for human masters, since you know that you will receive an inheritance from the Lord as a reward.

—Colossians 3:23-24 (NIV)

honor

 Success without honor is an unseasoned dish; it will satisfy your hunger, but it won't taste good.

—Joe Paterno

There's something distasteful about success without honor, **BusyCoach**. Winning games and championships generates excitement. But any success achieved without telling the truth, treating players fairly or following the rules, leaves a bittersweet aftertaste.

Although spectators may perceive you as honorable, only you know if it's true. Do you look yourself in the mirror each day with a clear conscience, knowing that you walked with honesty, fairness and integrity? How would those who work with you behind closed doors rate you on an honor scale?

Seek success at any cost, and you may get it; but it's sure to leave a bad taste in your mouth. Cultivate an honorable life, and you'll not only find lingering satisfaction, but also the sweet taste of success.

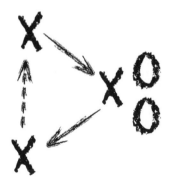

How will you live honorably today?

And what do you benefit if you gain the whole world but lose your own soul? Is anything worth more than your soul?

—Matthew 16:26

growth

 The leader's growth determines the people's growth.
—John Maxwell

Most **BusyCoach**es are in it to see their players grow as athletes and people. You attend clinics to stay on the cutting edge and teach the latest techniques. Your players engage with the community to experience the joy of helping others. You provide tutors and academic advisors to help them excel scholastically.

And yet sometimes you neglect your own growth. Not when it comes to technical knowledge about your sport, but rather knowledge about soft skills like effective delegation, emotional intelligence or people management.

Leaders who are growing inspire others to get better, too. As your players and staff see you pursuing professional and personal improvement, they will be encouraged to do the same.

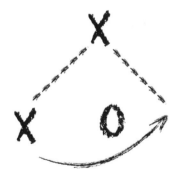

How are you growing in the soft skills of leadership?

And Jesus grew in wisdom and stature, and in favor with God and all the people.

—*Luke 2:52*

self-awareness

 Learning what you cannot do is more important than knowing what you can do.

—Lucille Ball

No one (including **BusyCoach**es) is gifted at Every. Single. Thing. You bring many strengths to the table. A big part of self-awareness is knowing them. Equally important is identifying the things you don't do well.

Excellent leaders surround themselves with people who fill in their gaps. If you don't excel at X's and O's, have a quality strategist on your staff. Not the best at reading the temperature of the team? Hire someone with high relational awareness. Scouting competition not your cup of tea? Fill that gap with someone who loves it.

Your limitations present an opportunity for the team. Surround yourself with staff who complement you and give them ownership of areas that align with their strengths. You get more done. And they feel valued, their motivation soars, and your team becomes stronger.

How are you developing the leaders around you?

Each time he said, "My grace is all you need. My power works best in weakness." So now I am glad to boast about my weaknesses, so that the power of Christ can work through me.

—*2 Corinthians 12:9*

purpose

 The measure of a life, after all, is not its duration but its donation.
—Corrie Ten Boom

Most of us measure life in years, **BusyCoach**. But our contribution to the world isn't determined by the length of time we get on Earth. Like me, you probably know people whose lives were short in years and long on influence.

Don't be fooled into thinking that older and wiser equals a greater donation to the world. All of us are prone to using our age or experience as excuses to just get by. Plenty of people have wasted days, months and years making little or no meaningful contribution to the world.

Let's be more concerned with impact than with longevity! Resist leaning on your years and experience as indicators of the size of your contribution.

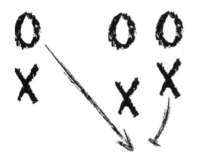 What opportunity for greater impact will you embrace today?

Be wise in the way you act toward outsiders; make the most of every opportunity.

—Colossians 4:5 (NIV)

risk

 All life is the management of risk, not its elimination.

—Walter Wriston

Can you imagine life without risk, **BusyCoach**? Safe, but incredibly boring! Some try to eliminate risk by becoming control freaks. Control is an illusion. A diagnosis, a destructive storm or a divisive team member quickly demonstrates just how little control we have.

You can't get rid of risk, but you can minimize it with solid planning, willing flexibility and excellent decision-making.

Planning gives you a template from which to work. Flexibility allows you to adjust to the unexpected—when your starting center gets mono, your co-worker resigns days before the season or your dad has a heart attack.

And then in the moment you make the best decision you can, you won't know all that you want to—that's what makes it a risk—but move ahead anyway.

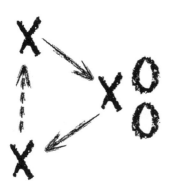

What risk are you managing today?

So Peter went over the side of the boat and walked on the water toward Jesus.

—*Matthew 14:29b*

action

 Ideas won't keep: something must be done about them.
—Alfred North Whitehead

Maybe you've participated in or even led brainstorming sessions or strategic planning meetings, **BusyCoach**. Inspiring ideas surface, momentum increases and individuals leave with renewed energy to move forward. Yet sometimes beneath the positivity, questions and hesitations lurk.

Will these ideas develop into something? Will we follow through to see them become reality? Will the time invested in brainstorming bear fruit?

Ideas are like fresh fruit or vegetables. If you and your team don't act on them, they will rot. But if you put those ideas into action and create something, they will provide just the right nutrition and energy to keep your team moving toward its goals.

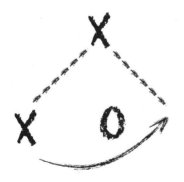

What new idea will you act on today?

"But you all came to me and said, 'First, let's send out scouts to explore the land for us. They will advise us on the best route to take and which towns we should enter.' "This seemed like a good idea to me, so I chose twelve scouts, one from each of your tribes."

—*Deuteronomy 1:22-23*

potential

 Focus on your potential instead of your limitations.
—Alan Loy McGinnis

We all have gaps, **BusyCoach**. Skills that just don't come naturally. Areas that take more time, effort and energy to manage.

Although we benefit from improving them, studies show that we go further, faster, by focusing more on our strengths—skills that do come naturally and more dramatically impact our potential for greatness.

The challenge is adopting strategies to minimize our gaps without becoming so focused (or discouraged!) that we neglect maximizing our strengths and becoming our best selves.

Let your strengths guide the roles and responsibilities you take on, and you'll be on the fast-track to reaching your potential.

Which of your strengths will help you win the day?

God has given each of you a gift from his great variety of spiritual gifts. Use them well to serve one another.

—1 Peter 4:10

impact

 You can impress people at a distance, but you can impact them only up close.

—Howard Hendricks

Do you seek to impress or impact, **BusyCoach**? To impress, keep your distance. Never let your guard down or admit your mistakes. Take an all-business approach to leading your team and, as the saying goes, "Never let them see you sweat."

If you desire to truly impact your players, then tear down your protective walls and let them get to know you. Admit your weaknesses and own your mistakes.

Share your truest self with your players—your favorite ice cream, pet peeves, values and dreams. Your vulnerability will create trust: the prerequisite to impacting people in meaningful, lasting ways.

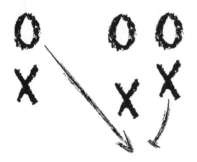

Open your heart in this way and watch the ripple effect it has on your team!

Oh, dear Corinthian friends! We have spoken honestly with you, and our hearts are open to you.

—2 Corinthians 6:11

opportunity

 Do what you can, with what you
have, where you are.

—Theodore Roosevelt

The grass is always greener, **BusyCoach**. You can always find a coach who has a bigger budget, better facilities or more staff. This comparison game typically results in frustration, complaining and excuses.

Instead, stay present in the moment and make the most of your current situation. You may not be able to do all that you want to, but you can do something. You may want more resources, but you have some. You may long for your dream job, but there's a purpose in your current one.

Refuse to squander the opportunity you have today. Be the best you can be where you are, and the future will take care of itself.

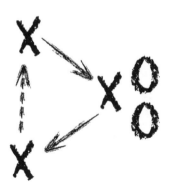

What will it take for you to stay present today?

"The master was full of praise. 'Well done, my good and faithful servant. You have been faithful in handling this small amount, so now I will give you many more responsibilities. Let's celebrate together!'"

—*Matthew 25:21*

teamwork

 Alone we can do so little;
together we can do so much.
—Helen Keller

Teamwork is such a beautiful thing, **BusyCoach**! Deep satisfaction comes from joining with others to achieve a common goal. Few feelings compare!

Yet sometimes it's easier to do it all yourself—to think you've got to be the star recruiter, scouter, strategist, and more, in order to win. Instead, you end up a stress ball with burnout and health issues.

Trying to do it all leads to resentment. Delegate responsibilities to staff in light of their maturity and experience, and let them give it a go. With your supervision and coaching, they will learn, and you will find a better rhythm. Plus, the team will achieve so much more!

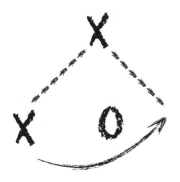

What tasks can you delegate this week?

The eye can never say to the hand, "I don't need you." The head can't say to the feet, "I don't need you."

—1 Corinthians 12:21

gratitude

Maybe [cancer] is the greatest blessing of all.

—Kay Yow

That quote may catch you off guard, **BusyCoach**. Kay Yow spoke those words back in 2008. They struck me then, and still do today. She called the cancer that brought her so much pain and suffering a blessing? How could this be?

Coach Yow lived with gratitude despite her circumstances. She saw how cancer allowed her to reach more people with her message of hope and encouragement. And how it led to the inception of the Kay Yow Cancer Fund, which has raised millions for research on women's cancers.

She saw a bigger picture. Even in the worst of times, she found something good—a silver lining in a dark cloud. You can too. No matter what your situation, take time to reflect on all the good in your life and give thanks.

How will you practice gratitude today?

Be thankful in all circumstances, for this is God's will for you who belong to Christ Jesus.

—1 Thessalonians 5:18

example

People do what people see.
They forget your words but
follow your footsteps.
—John Maxwell

Your players are more interested in what you do than what you say, **BusyCoach**. For your words to hold water, you must follow them up with supporting actions.

You probably tell your players to respect one another. That's good! But if they hear you disrespect an assistant, video coordinator or bus driver, you're basically giving them the OK to treat others disrespectfully.

Hopefully, you encourage your players to work things out with people in a productive and courteous manner. But if they see you doing the opposite, like talking about unresolved conflict with a third party, you can be sure they'll follow your example and not your words.

The more your words line up with your actions, the more likely your players will do what you say.

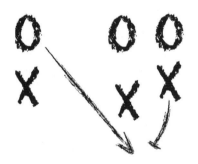

How well do your words and actions match?

So Jesus explained, "I tell you the truth, the Son can do nothing by himself. He does only what he sees the Father doing. Whatever the Father does, the Son also does."

—John 5:19

leadership

Great leaders reframe what
a win looks like.

—Robert Nagle

Sometimes the season throws you a curveball, **BusyCoach**. Maybe a lot of curveballs! These come in all shapes and sizes— player injuries, necessary disciplinary action or crises that affect your campus.

Situations like these may require mid-course corrections to your team goals. Perhaps winning the conference title is no longer realistic or statistical goals for each game need tweaking. Sometimes a win isn't measured by the scoreboard, but by incremental improvement or getting closer to achieving the revised goals.

Quality leaders aren't afraid to make these kinds of adjustments. As the team finds success in attaining these new goals, it will pick up momentum and confidence to keep moving forward.

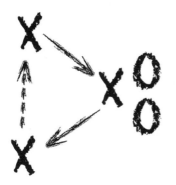

Which of your team goals need tweaking?

All athletes are disciplined in their training. They do it to win a prize that will fade away, but we do it for an eternal prize.

—1 Corinthians 9:25

consistency

Building a high-performance organization starts with who you are every day for your team.
—Robyn Benincasa

Every. Single. Day. is so important, **BusyCoach**. Building a championship program comes down to not only what you do each day for your team, but also—and more importantly—who you are each day to your team.

Consistent leaders create a culture in which team members know what to expect. Moody leaders cause uncertainty as staff and players wonder which coach will show up. This tense culture inhibits everyone, including the leader, from performing at their best.

What will it take for you to bring your best self to your team every day? Do you need exercise to eliminate stress? Quiet time to read or pray each morning? A date night with your spouse every week?

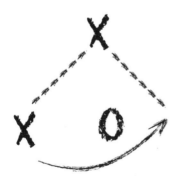

Do whatever it takes. Your team's performance depends on it.

Oh, that my actions would consistently reflect your decrees!

—*Psalm 119:5*

wisdom

The desire to reach for the stars is ambitious. The desire to reach hearts is wise.

—Maya Angelou

You wouldn't be in the profession if you weren't reaching for the stars, **BusyCoach**! All the external measurements of success—wins, championships, graduation rates—are worth reaching for and satisfying to achieve. There's certainly nothing wrong with those ambitions!

Even more gratifying though is reaching the heart of your players. To focus not only on the results you believe they can achieve, but also on their personal growth and development.

Loving them where they are, extending grace when they mess up and speaking truth when they need to be held accountable. This is what will reach their hearts.

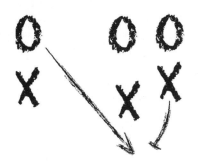

What will you do to reach their hearts this week?

The purposes of a person's heart are deep waters, but one who has insight draws them out.

—Proverbs 20:5 (NIV)

preparation

 A company is like a ship.
Everyone ought to be
prepared to take the helm.
—Morris Weeks

How are you equipping others to take the helm if you should need to step away, **BusyCoach**?

Life happens, even during the season. Coaches can have heart problems or strokes, lose spouses or parents, or even get fired—all in the middle of the season. No one ever thought it would happen to them.

What will happen to your team if something takes you out of commission? Or, as an assistant, how are you preparing yourself if a predicament arises that requires you to step up and lead? The time to prepare for these events is before they happen, not after.

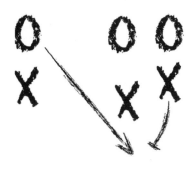

What will you do today so your team will still excel in the midst of a tough situation?

Preach the word; be prepared in season and out of season; correct, rebuke and encourage—with great patience and careful instruction.

—2 Timothy 4:2 (NIV)

change

Everyone starts strong. Success comes to those with unwavering commitment to be at the end.
—Howard Schultz

What needs to change, **BusyCoach**? Not just for your team but for your life?

You know the dismal stats about New Year's resolutions. People get off to a strong start but begin to fade when things get tough or life gets in the way. In weeks or sometimes just days, old habits resurface.

A key to reaching your goals is having a clear vision of what you want life to look like in a year, as well as the discipline to revisit that vision weekly, if not daily. Many give up because they forget their why. Frequent reminders of your big-picture vision will keep you going when you want to give up.

Let that vision drive your commitment to the daily and weekly changes that will take you to new places!

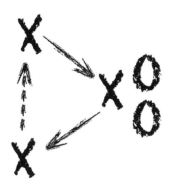

What vision are you pursuing?

I have fought the good fight, I have finished the race, and I have remained faithful.

—*2 Timothy 4:7*

possibility

Most of the things worth doing in the world had been declared impossible before they were done.

—Louis D. Brandeis

What seems impossible, **BusyCoach**? Getting to 20 wins? Landing a lynchpin recruit? Finishing your master's degree?

Think of all the people who heard it couldn't be done— Abraham Lincoln, the Wright Brothers, Mother Teresa, Pat Summitt. Imagine our world without their influence, invention or presence!

Achieving your impossibilities will make a difference in a life, a community, a world. Along the way though you'll hear your internal whisperings (and those of others) of doubt that seek to distract and discourage you.

The great ones have learned to speak to themselves rather than listen to themselves. Whether the dissenting voices surface from inside or outside, combat them with the truth and keep moving.

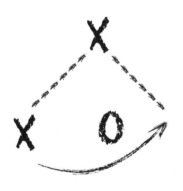

What impossibilities will you prove possible?

Jesus looked at them intently and said, "Humanly speaking it is impossible. But with God everything is possible."

—*Luke 1:37*

rest

 Give me six hours to chop
down a tree and I will spend the
first four sharpening the axe.
—Abraham Lincoln

This seems counter-productive doesn't it, **BusyCoach**? In a world obsessed with multi-tasking and squeezing productivity out of every single minute, it seems the job would get done faster by jumping in and sawing away.

Wisdom speaks from a bigger picture. Using a sharp saw takes less effort than working with a dull one, so taking time to sharpen the saw makes reaching goals easier. You're working with the saw rather than fighting against it.

In life, sharpening the saw takes many forms, one of which is rest. I know, I know. You don't have time to rest! Yet, if you don't find ways to rest your body and mind (especially during the season), you can't possibly give your team your best. Eventually, you'll be running on fumes!

Don't just work harder. Work smarter. Take time to sharpen your saw!

Then, because so many people were coming and going that they did not even have a chance to eat, [Jesus] said to them, "Come with me by yourselves to a quiet place and get some rest."

—Mark 6:31

toughness

 You are not tough alone.
—Mike Krzyzewski

BusyCoaches are tough. You're driven and determined. You push through hardship and discouragement. You refuse to let defeat get the best of you.

But it's hard to be tough alone. Left by yourself, thoughts of doubt go from whispers to shouts. Discouragement looms overhead. Defeat feels bigger and darker.

Locking arms with a co-worker, colleague or family member helps diffuse the doubt, discouragement or defeat. A word of encouragement, a selfless act or even just a smile offers hope. Gives perspective. Renews energy.

This is true for both you and your players. A culture of unity is imperative to developing greater toughness.

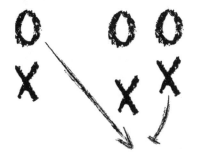

Stay together to stay tough!

How good and pleasant it is when God's people live together in unity!

—Psalm 133:1

greatness

One of the marks of true greatness is the ability to develop greatness in others.

—J.C. McCauley

When it comes to coaching, we usually equate greatness with the number of games won, **BusyCoach**. The best coaches, however, win much more than just games. Their biggest wins come in the form of helping others identify and use their unique strengths.

Authentic greatness is others-centered. It's being more concerned for a co-worker or a player's growth than our own success. It's investing time and creating opportunity for others to succeed.

Great coaches see others not for who they are today, but for who they can become. When we see signs of greatness in the people around us, and then inspire and encourage it to develop, we achieve greatness, too.

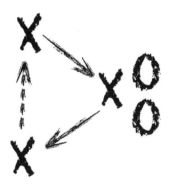

Who are your players becoming?

Let us think of ways to motivate one another to acts of love and good works.

—*Hebrews 10:24*

friendship

 A true friend is someone who
can make us do what we can.
—Ralph Waldo Emerson

We all need some true friends with whom to journey though life, **BusyCoach**. We weren't made to walk the windy and sometimes bumpy path alone. It feels lonely and discouraging.

A true friend provides so much. A listening yet non-judgmental ear when we need to vent. A forgiving heart when we mess up. An encouraging word when we want to throw in the towel.

We possess much more potential than we realize. Many of us barely scratch the surface of our capabilities. Yet the camaraderie and encouragement of a true friend can spur us on to our greatness and our very best selves!

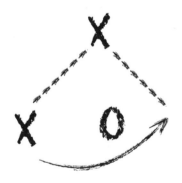

Thank your friends today for the ways they bless you!

As iron sharpens iron, so a friend sharpens a friend.

—*Proverbs 27:17*

entitlement

Entitlement never wins championships. Investment wins championships.
—Kevin Eastman

The word "entitlement" pops up everywhere, **BusyCoach**. We use its most basic definition—the fact of having a right to something—to describe the next generation. But I see it in people everywhere—including in the mirror.

The entitled speak in terms of what's deserved regardless of time and effort put forth. We deserve success because of our social status, the school name on our chest or our God-given talent.

The invested, on the other hand, recognize the road to success is paved with hard work. Champions know that fully investing in a team, cause or purpose bigger than themselves requires consistent commitment, selflessness and perseverance.

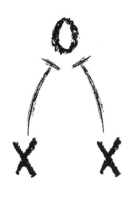

Steer clear of an entitled mindset by continuing to invest the hard work that leads the way to championships!

All hard work brings a profit, but mere talk leads only to poverty.

—*Proverbs 14:23 (NIV)*

action

 Trying times are not the
times to stop trying.

—Ray Owen

Tough times can paralyze us, **BusyCoach**. Life is challenging and just plain hard. Even Pat Summitt has talked about the days after her Alzheimer's diagnosis when she crawled in bed and pulled the sheets over her head.

It happens to the best of us. (And, honestly, it made me feel better to know that even Pat had days like that!) It's human nature to want to quit. To throw in the towel. What makes champions so special is that they resist this human response and refuse to stop trying.

Some days it's just like Pat taught her son, Tyler: Right foot, left foot, breathe. It's one step, one action at a time.

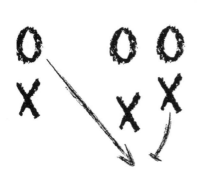

Whatever hardship you face today, chase greatness by resolving to keep moving, one small step at a time!

The righteous keep moving forward, and those with clean hands become stronger and stronger.

—Job 17:9

growth

The man who does not
read good books has no
advantage over the man
who can't read them.

— Mark Twain

Successful people enjoy learning, **BusyCoach**. And usually that means reading (or listening to) books. Pat Williams, Senior Vice President of the Orlando Magic, may be an extreme example, reading five to six books at a time with a goal of finishing one book a day.

Perhaps that seems as out of reach for you as it does for me! But even for those with lesser reading goals, the No. 1 excuse for not getting it done is—you guessed it—busyness.

If you want to grow then carve out the time to read, even if it's just 10 to 15 minutes at a time. Name one book you want to read but haven't. Today is the day.

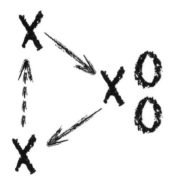

Make a choice to add reading to your day and watch your leadership flourish.

The wise are mightier than the strong, and those with knowledge grow stronger and stronger.

—Proverbs 24:5

persective

 In spite of everything, I still
believe people are really
good at heart.

—Anne Frank

What if we believed this too, **BusyCoach**? Anne Frank saw such atrocity, and she still saw something good in humankind.

We're quick to make up things about someone and what they do. Inaccurate judgments seldom take into account the path that individual walked, and the joys and disappointments that shaped him.

What if instead we saw good in their heart? How would it impact our interactions with the player who is struggling academically? An overly negative colleague? The parent who won't speak to us since we cut her child's playing time?

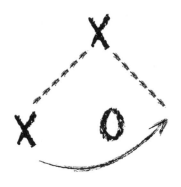

Less judgment. More grace. Better relation- ships. Let's give it a try!

I know, my God, that you examine our hearts and rejoice when you find integrity there.

—1 Chronicles 29:17a

courage

 Life shrinks or expands in
proportion to one's courage.
—Anas Nin

Living large requires courage, **BusyCoach**. But doubts surface as you strive for your goals. Do I have what it takes? What if I fail? Am I good enough?

Courage isn't the absence of doubts, but the ability to focus and press on in spite of them. There's no more powerful example than the life of Louis Zamperini.

Olympic track star turned bombardier, Zamperini lived through a plane crash that left him stranded on a raft for 47 days surrounded by sharks, only to be captured by the Japanese and tortured in POW camps for more than two years. His story, told in the book and movie *Unbroken*, is one of undying courage, will power and determination.

Our military heroes live huge lives as they demonstrate courage again and again in the face of the most dire circumstances. Though our context is much different, may we combat the doubt and fear we face today with the same courage to overcome.

What doubts and fear will you press through today?

So be strong and courageous! Do not be afraid and do not panic before them. For the LORD your God will personally go ahead of you. He will neither fail you nor abandon you.

—Deuteronomy 31:6

humility

Accepting help is a gift to the helper.

—Robyn Benincasa

Many leaders thrive on being able to do it all, **BusyCoach**. Society teaches that those who don't or can't are a step slow and a dollar short. They just don't measure up.

The opposite is actually true. Leaders who accept help create synergy with their co-workers. This simple act communicates that each person has something valuable to contribute to the team goals and objectives. Every time you accept help, you give someone else on your team a chance to shine.

Resist the lie that accepting help means you're weak! It actually shows strength and humility to admit you can't do it all, which in turn promotes teamwork and unity.

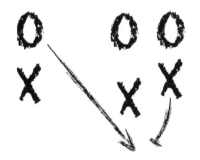

From whom will you receive help today?

Share each other's burdens, and in this way obey the law of Christ.

—*Galatians 6:2*

adversity

The best way out is always through.

—Robert Frost

What a difficult truth, **BusyCoach**. Whatever we're facing—an injury, a broken relationship, a difficult work environment—the way to greener pastures is through it, not around it.

We want an out. A way to avoid the pain and discomfort of going "through." Although the way around is longer, many times we persist in taking that route.

Going through is hard. It hurts—so much that we may feel like giving up. Going around may feel less painful, but may yield fewer results. If we want that injured body part, relationship or work environment to reach its maximum strength and potential, we've got to go through.

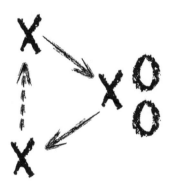

What will you choose to go through rather than around?

Even when I walk through the darkest valley, I will not be afraid, for you are close beside me.

—Psalm 23:4

serve

I began learning long ago that those who are happiest are those who do the most for others.

—Booker T. Washington

You're probably familiar with the concept of boundaries, **BusyCoach**. Much like a fence that borders physical property, our boundaries delineate that for which we are and are not responsible. Yet, like wind that blows your neighbors leaves into your yard, many circumstances for which we are not responsible do impact us.

Though you may not be responsible for a player's injury, a booster's actions or a staff member's behavior, you are responsible for how you respond to it. That's in your yard. And your response is a choice.

You choose whether to lose your cool or to stay calm. Whether to get stuck or to keep moving. Whether to become discouraged or to rise above.

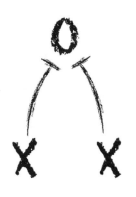

The best leaders respond to tough circumstances with poise, positivity and the resolve to press through them.

For we are each responsible for our own conduct.

—*Galatians 6:5*

gratitude

The more you complain,
the more you find things to
complain about. The more you
give thanks, the more you find
things to be thankful for.

—Anonymous

Some call it the law of attraction, **BusyCoach**. Like when we get a new car and suddenly see the same make and model everywhere. We become more aware of that upon which we focus.

When we see the world through a negative lens, we see obstacles and deficiencies around every corner. The more you complain about your lack of resources, unsupportive boss or health challenges, the more overwhelming they become.

The same principle applies when we maintain a spirit of gratitude. See life through a thankful lens and suddenly you notice the multitude of people, circumstances and opportunities for which you can give thanks. Most tough situations have a silver lining. Even in the midst of discouragement, disease or destruction, we can find one.

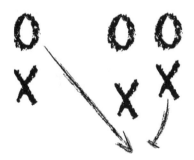

Choose gratitude and watch a world of blessings open up to you.

I will give thanks to you, Lord, with all my heart; I will tell of all your wonderful deeds.

—Psalm 9:1 (NIV)

leadership

 Leaders don't create followers,
they create more leaders.
—Tom Peters

This is the heart of leadership, **BusyCoach**. Not to amass throngs of followers, but to multiply your life in such a way that teaches others how to lead. This takes a proactive, intentional approach.

Many **BusyCoach**es want players to step up as leaders but few take the time to give them the tools to understand how. Clearly explain your expectations—it's impossible to do this too often! Help them assess their leadership strengths and areas of needed growth.

Teach them what it looks like to lead by example and with their voice. Model for them how to resolve conflict or to approach difficult conversations with teammates.

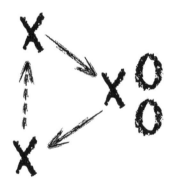

What action will you take to invest in your team leaders?

You have heard me teach things that have been confirmed by many reliable witnesses. Now teach these truths to other trustworthy people who will be able to pass them on to others.

—2 Timothy 2:2

attitude

Your attitude is either the lock
or the key to the door of success.
—Anonymous

Few things make and break the journey toward success like attitude, **BusyCoach**.

Like me, you've probably observed men and women whose positive attitudes catapulted them over adversity or helped them to accomplish amazing feats despite lacking physical talent. At the same time, a person doesn't have to look too far or wide to see coaches and players who sabotage their remarkable talent with unremarkable attitudes.

The most inspiring among us are those who refuse to allow their circumstances to lock them out of success. They continually find a new perspective, a ray of hope, an alternative route, that helps them keep a positive outlook. It's not rocket science, but it does require proactive tenacity to stay positive in tough times.

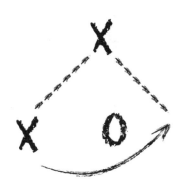

How will your attitude today open the door to future success?

Serve with a good attitude, as to the Lord and not to men...

   —Ephesians 6:7 (HCSB)

toughness

Competitive toughness is an acquired skill and not an inherited gift.

—Chris Evert

It's tempting to think that toughness is a quality players either have or don't have, **BusyCoach**. An innate wiring; like being an extrovert or introvert, thinker or feeler, linear or intuitive. It's simply part of their DNA.

The truth is, toughness—whether in competition or in life—can be taught. It's not set in stone. Rather, it's a trait that players and coaches can develop. Anyone can become tougher.

At its core, toughness is about getting comfortable being uncomfortable. For the **BusyCoach**, it may mean embracing conflict and having the difficult conversation with a player, administrator or parent. Or perhaps it's sticking with an exercise regimen during the season. Or becoming more open or vulnerable with a family member or friend.

Getting tougher requires experiencing discomfort and choosing to stay in it instead of running for your life. With practice, the uncomfortableness becomes more tolerable, and your toughness muscle grows.

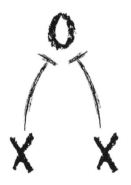

In what ways are you developing more toughness?

A final word: Be strong in the Lord and in his mighty power.

—Ephesians 6:10

integrity

 The time is always right to
do what is right.
—Martin Luther King, Jr.

The complexities of life in the 21st century abound, **BusyCoach**! The advances of our day in technology and innovation are mind-boggling. The debates over issues like health care, discrimination or pay for college athletes don't have easy answers.

In the midst of all the complexity, simplicity exists. At the core of our humanity we know what's right. It's right to treat others with dignity and respect. It's right to abide by the law. It's right to speak truthfully in love.

Players are watching and following your lead. Set the example you want them to emulate.

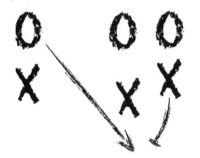

Today and every day, do what is right.

...the Lord has told you what is good, and this is what he requires of you: to do what is right, to love mercy, and to walk humbly with your God.

—Micah 6:8

sacrifice

 Great achievement is usually
born of great sacrifice…
—Napoleon Hill

You're aware of the sacrifices that accompany achievement, **BusyCoach**. You know private sacrifice always precedes public victory.

Olympians who master their craft make it look so easy to achieve greatness. Most people can't fully grasp the grueling workouts, intense mental training and years of personal sacrifice they (and their families) willingly make. As you well know, the journey to the top is incredibly tough!

Though sacrifice doesn't guarantee a victory or gold medal, it's still worth it for all that it develops within us. You and your players invest hundreds (if not thousands) of hours planning and training for competition. No matter the final score...

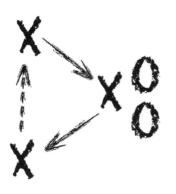

you'll always come out ahead when you willingly train and sacrifice to become your very best.

Let us not become weary in doing good, for at the proper time we will reap a harvest if we do not give up.

—Galatians 6:9

comparison

 Comparison is the thief of joy.
—Theodore Roosevelt

It's so easy to make comparisons, isn't it **BusyCoach**? Many of us constantly eye how we measure up in terms of wins, losses, salaries, weight—you name it. Some say these comparisons motivate us to keep striving for excellence. Yet comparison can also result in discontentment and frustration.

Ultimately, success isn't found in getting more than the next person. Its essence isn't a dollar figure or square footage. As John Wooden defined it, success is about being "the best that you are capable of becoming."

You will lose sight of your own values and purpose if you constantly look over your shoulder to compare yourself to other coaches. You'll forget who you are and whom you want to be.

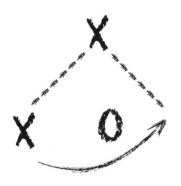

True joy is found in the self-satisfaction of becoming your best.

Pay careful attention to your own work, for then you will get the satisfaction of a job well done, and you won't need to compare yourself to anyone else.

—*Galatians 6:4*

courage

Leading others takes courage. Knowing the right decision is usually easy. Making the right decision is hard.

—John Maxwell

It takes courage to be a **BusyCoach**. To stand for what's right even when you feel like you're standing alone. To confront a litany of daily decisions, the consequences of which touch many, many lives. To hold your head high in the face of adversity, criticism and discouragement.

Oftentimes you know what to do, but can't pull the trigger. At some point, more information or debate with trustworthy advisors becomes counter-productive. If you've done your due diligence, mulling it around longer may only bring more confusion.

This is the moment of truth—the moment where courage must triumph over fear!

Make the best
decision you can
with what you
know today.

This is my command—be strong and courageous! Do not be afraid or discouraged. For the Lord your God is with you wherever you go.

—Joshua 1:9

leadership

The art of leadership is saying
no, not yes. It is very easy to
say yes.

—Tony Blair

BusyCoaches tend to have a high capacity to juggle a number of responsibilities. You want to do it all and be all things to all people.

Surely you've been confronted with the impossibility of this do it all, be it all mentality. It's not only unrealistic, but unhealthy—paving the way to becoming overwhelmed and eventually burned-out. There's a two-fold antidote.

First, use your vision, mission and values to determine the activities and opportunities most important to your stated purpose. This helps you to focus on the best while saying no to the rest.

Second, become a delegating machine. Are there responsibilities only you can perform? What can you pass-off? Give staff, grad assistants and managers more responsibility and ownership. This win-win increases your effectiveness and at the same time provides valuable training to others.

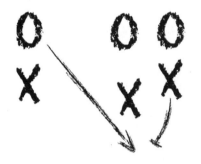

How will you say no this week?

"This is not good!" Moses' father-in-law exclaimed. "You're going to wear yourself out—and the people, too. This job is too heavy a burden for you to handle all by yourself. "

   —Exodus 18:17-18

action

Start by doing what's necessary, then what's possible, and suddenly you are doing the impossible.

—Saint Francis of Assisi

Ever feel stuck, **BusyCoach**? Like you know action is required, but you're not sure where to start? Maybe you've inherited a struggling program and feel overwhelmed with all the necessary changes. Or perhaps your team is so full of complainers and drama queens that you're not sure how to stop the bleeding.

When you don't know what to do, do the next right thing. Breaking it down and taking the first necessary action reduces the enormity of the overall task and gets you moving. Then do the next action—and the next, and the next.

You'll begin to see possibilities and gain momentum. Then suddenly, you and your team are doing what once looked impossible!

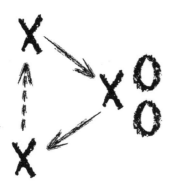

Remember, every journey begins with the first step.

Jesus replied, "What is impossible with man is possible with God."

—*Luke 18:27 (NIV)*

impact

 Education is the most powerful
weapon which you can use to
change the world.
                              —Nelson Mandela

BusyCoaches are in it to make a difference. As you affect the lives of your players—men and women who will likely become employees, spouses, parents and leaders—your contribution can truly change the world.

With a field or court as your classroom, you educate every single day. Although the X's and O's are important, the broader education you pass along is even more crucial.

Under your tutelage, your players learn how to work toward a common goal with others, how to push through adverse situations and how to stay disciplined when they don't feel like it. They will draw on these skills every day of their lives—long after their sporting careers have concluded.

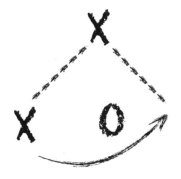

Be encouraged! You are training your athletes for life!

And you yourself must be an example to them by doing good works of every kind. Let everything you do reflect the integrity and seriousness of your teaching.

—Titus 2:7

loyalty

 To retain the loyalty of those who are present, be loyal to those who are absent.
                     —Stephen R. Covey

If anything is evident in this new age of technology, it's that our words are public, **BusyCoach**. Even the ones we speak to an individual or in a small staff meeting. Our words make or break loyalty.

When we communicate in a way that respects those not in the room, we demonstrate to those in the room that they can trust us; that in their absence, we will be loyal to them.

The flip side is also true. Nothing destroys loyalty faster than negative talk about people not present. Your audience imagines that you will talk about them in the same way when they aren't within earshot.

If you want deeper loyalty on your team, watch your words. They matter.

The hearts of the wise make their mouths prudent, and their lips promote instruction.

—*Proverbs 16:23 (NIV)*

teamwork

 I not only use all the brains
I have, but all I can borrow.
—Woodrow Wilson

The best leaders realize they don't know it all, **BusyCoach**. Rather, they facilitate a spirit of unity and teamwork by drawing on the wisdom, insight and intelligence of others.

Although some fear that this leaves them looking foolish or unqualified, the opposite happens—borrowing another's intellect actually makes you look smarter.

This humble approach creates buy-in by giving other team members a voice. Showing you value their role and contribution communicates trust. And people who feel trusted invest more and perform better.

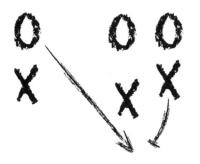

So if you want your team to get ahead, start borrowing some brains!

Plans go wrong for lack of advice; many advisers bring success.

—*Proverbs 15:22*

complaining

If you don't like something, change it. If you can't change it, change your attitude.
Don't complain.

—Maya Angelou

Complaining is like a little spark in a parched forest, **BusyCoach**. Just one complainer can singlehandedly destroy a team by setting a firestorm of negativity ablaze.

From time to time, we encounter people and situations we don't like; many of whom may be worthy of complaint. Whether global issues of injustice and inequality, or seemingly smaller inconveniences like flat tires and unfriendly cashiers, it's harder to find a needle in a haystack than to find something to complain about.

Though most things are outside our control, we DO have power over our attitude and words. Stay mindful of the negative message that complaining sends to your followers. Do all you can to pour water on any negative sparks that flare up.

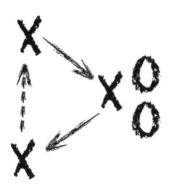

You may want your team to be on fire in many ways, but not this one!

Likewise, the tongue is a small part of the body, but it makes great boasts. Consider what a great forest is set on fire by a small spark.

—James 3:5 (NIV)

kindness

Be kind, for everyone you meet
is fighting a hard battle.
—Reverend John Watson

Every person you meet has a story, **BusyCoach**.
Every. Single. One.

Whether you find yourself out recruiting, on campus or in the grocery, each person with whom you interact experiences problems and challenges, just like you. Those battles take many forms like an argument with a loved one, depression or financial instability.

So, today, rather than passing a quick judgment, choose kindness. Remember that the behavior you see is likely a response to a battle being fought in the background of someone's life. Extend grace. Offer a smile, a kind word or a hand.

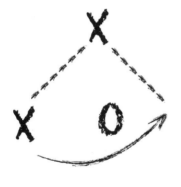

You never know how your kindness might change the trajectory of someone's day, week or even life!

Anxiety weighs down the heart, but a kind word cheers it up.

—Proverbs 12:25 (NIV)

smile

A smile remains the most inexpensive gift I can bestow on anyone and yet its powers can vanquish kingdoms.

—Og Mandino

We can make things more complicated than necessary, **BusyCoach**. Creating a healthy, positive and successful team culture can certainly be complex, but one strategy that's so often overlooked can help.

Quite simply, smile. You've probably heard that it takes more muscles to frown than to smile. Smiling also produces the antidepressant serotonin, which helps you feel more positive. And, as you know, positivity is contagious.

You don't have to hire a team building expert (although that's not a bad idea!) to give your team culture a positive shot in the arm. Just start with a smile.

Practice smiling more and see what happens!

When they were discouraged, I smiled at them. My look of approval was precious to them.

—Job 29:24

adversity

"" The difference between a successful person and others is not a lack of strength, not a lack of knowledge, but rather a lack of determination.

—Vince Lombardi

You'll come up against adversity this season, **BusyCoach**. An inopportune loss. A hyper-critical reporter. A difficult player relationship.

Achieving success in these situations may be less about fostering enough strength to push through or smarts to figure things out. Rather, success comes to those who just plain refuse to give up. To those determined enough to get up regardless of what knocks them down.

No matter what threatens to derail you today, be determined to not give up. Do the next right thing. Find the silver lining. Consider a different approach. And, in so doing, you'll show a generation of instant-gratification junkies one of the keys to becoming a successful person.

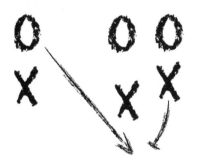

Keep going – your success, your victory, may be around the next corner.

We can rejoice, too, when we run into problems and trials, for we know that they help us develop endurance. And endurance develops strength of character, and character strengthens our confident hope of salvation.

—Romans 5:3-4

sowing

Always do your best. What you plant now, you will harvest later.
—Og Mandino

There's a principle that always holds true, **BusyCoach**. That of sowing and reaping. It's evident all around us.

Athletes who plant seeds like hard work and discipline enjoy the reward of becoming more skilled. Coaches who plant seeds of positivity, reap the benefit of creating an environment in which people love to work.

Unfortunately, this principle also exists with qualities you may not want to harvest. Sow distrust and others will return distrust. Plant seeds of anger and reap a hostile culture.

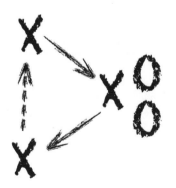

No matter what you're shooting for, what you plant today will determine your harvest!

A man reaps what he sows.

   —Galatians 6:7b

wisdom

To know what you know and to know what you don't know, that is real wisdom.

—Confucius

Know-it-alls don't make fantastic leaders, **BusyCoach**.
In fact, most of us don't even enjoy working with—let alone
following—people who think they know everything about
everything.

None of us know everything. Folks who think they do are
tough to follow because they lack the authenticity to own up
to the truth.

But we eagerly follow leaders humble enough to admit their
faults because their honesty reminds us that they're just like
us—imperfect people who don't know it all!

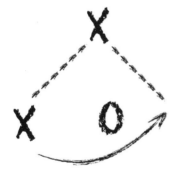

The best
leaders know
their strengths
and freely
admit what they
don't know.

*"Where were you when I laid the foundations of the earth? Tell me, if you
know so much."*

—Job 38:4

example

Children have never been very good at listening to their elders, but they have never failed to imitate them.

–James Baldwin

So many of us, **BusyCoach**, have uttered the words, "Do what I say, not what I do." Though it's much easier to speak words of instruction than to live them out, it's not nearly as effective.

Your leadership rests heavily on your behaviors. If you tell your players that their words matter, but they see you verbally demean people, they'll follow your actions. If you tell them they need to show self-control in the heat of the battle, and then they watch you lose your mind during a lousy practice, guess which message they remember?

Which behaviors this past week would you be proud to have your players imitate? Which ones, if imitated, would embarrass you?

Even small adjustments in your actions will glean big rewards in your team culture!

Live a life filled with love, following the example of Christ.

—Ephesians 5:2a

failure

 People who avoid failure
also avoid success.
—Robert Kiyosaki

Most of the players you coach are afraid to fail, **BusyCoach**. Many have received so much applause and so many trophies that even a minor setback has a devastating effect.

Reinforce daily that failure is part of success—a necessary stop on the road to greatness. Although playing it safe feels comfortable, the discomfort of mistakes will accelerate their growth as athletes and people.

How you respond to their mistakes is crucial. Go ballistic, and they'll play tight for fear of messing up. But respond as a composed teacher, and you'll help them understand that the world won't fall off its axis because they missed the goal or dropped the pass. They'll stay loose and perform better.

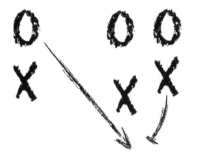

How will you teach your players to handle mistakes?

Even youths will become weak and tired, and young men will fall in exhaustion. But those who trust in the LORD will find new strength. They will soar high on wings like eagles. They will run and not grow weary. They will walk and not faint.

—Isaiah 40:30-31

potential

There is no passion to be found playing small – in settling for a life that is less than the one you are capable of living.

—Nelson Mandela

You're capable of so much more than you think, **BusyCoach**. Just ask a U.S. Navy Seal or an ultra-marathoner.

You challenge your players to give more, knowing their bodies can endure more than their minds believe. You constantly seek new methods of motivation to push them beyond their perceived breaking point.

Anyone is susceptible to this "playing small," even you. Avoiding the conflict with a colleague in your department, hoping it will disappear. Allowing your fear of public speaking to keep you from marketing your team in the community. Holding back that new idea from your head coach because you might look foolish.

Stretch yourself this week to play bigger and discover your greater potential!

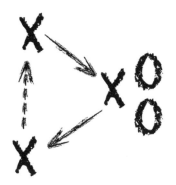

Where are you playing small?

Daniel soon proved himself more capable than all the other administrators and high officers. Because of Daniel's great ability, the king made plans to place him over the entire empire.

—Daniel 6:3

gratitude

Feeling gratitude and not expressing it is like wrapping a present and not giving it.
—William Arthur Ward

We tend to be ultra-conscious of our blessings at the end of November, **BusyCoach**. During the week of Thanksgiving, many of us share the things for which we are most thankful. Of all the 52 weeks of the year, this is the one week in which those feelings may actually find their expression in words.

The challenge is to consciously express gratitude during the other 51 weeks—by not only recognizing our blessings, but also giving others an amazing gift by verbalizing them!

Affirming others breathes life into their soul and refreshes us at the same time.

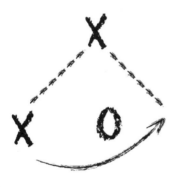

Let's not end up with a bunch of wrapped presents. Let's give them away every week of the year.

Enter his gates with thanksgiving; go into his courts with praise. Give thanks to him and praise his name.

—Psalm 100:4

growth

 The greatest oak was once a little nut who held its ground.
—Author Unknown

BusyCoaches strive to build excellent, strong programs. You may start out small, but you seek growth that will lead to conference or perhaps national prominence.

Many of the same ingredients required for a little nut to become a huge oak tree are just as important to your team's growth—time, nurturing, patience and the right nutrients. When storms come along (and they will), rushing, controlling or hijacking the process never yields the best results.

Believe in the process. Stay patient with the process. Keep providing the encouragement and correction necessary to the process.

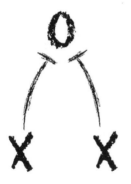

Stay the course and with persistence, your team will grow strong like that big old oak tree!

It's not important who does the planting, or who does the watering. What's important is that God makes the seed grow.

—1 Corinthians 3:7

influence

> There are only two ways to influence human behavior: you can manipulate it or you can inspire it.
>
> —Simon Sinek

*BusyCoach*es everywhere want to know how to motivate their players. Executing strategy, maintaining focus, competing passionately: The art of coaching is all about influencing athletes to give and become more than they think they can.

Many use manipulative techniques like fear to accomplish the task. Although manipulation works in the short term, it doesn't create lasting change. The best way to do that is through inspiration.

Determine WHY your athletes play and you'll find a key to influencing their behavior for longer intervals. Inspire them in the direction of their WHY and you're more likely to get what you want—stronger, more consistent performance.

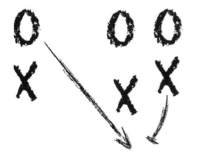

Do you know why your athletes compete?

A good leader motivates, doesn't mislead, doesn't exploit.

   —Proverbs 16:10 (MSG)

authenticity

 It isn't what you do, it's how you do it.

—John Wooden

As the saying goes, there are a thousand ways to skin a cat, **BusyCoach**. And just as many approaches to coaching. It's not so much *that* you perform the duties of a coach, but rather *how* you perform them.

Coaches carry-out similar tasks—teaching, recruiting, strategizing and leading teams. Yet, of the throngs of coaches in the world, there's only one YOU. And remaining true to yourself— your values, beliefs and style—is crucial in finding success. Learn tips from mentor coaches, but stay authentic to you.

Take inventory of all the coaches who've won championships in your sport and you'll find a myriad of approaches. A coach once told me that she wasn't sure she could win a title coaching the way she liked to coach. I assured her that coaching her way was her best chance!

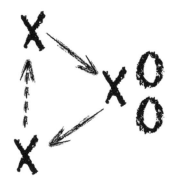

Remember, coach in a way that reflects your core values and beliefs.

Thank you for making me so wonderfully complex! Your workmanship is marvelous—how well I know it.

—Psalm 139:14

attention

A wealth of information creates a poverty of attention.
—Herbert Simon

We are a distracted people, **BusyCoach**. Inundated daily by thousands of messages, tweets, posts, commercials, articles, blogs, and so much more. Though wonderful conveniences, our phones, tablets and computers have resulted in an addiction to information that can negatively impact our relationships.

We may be with people, but we're not really *with* them. The millennials aren't the only ones with minuscule attention spans—it's all of us. There's no faster way to de-value someone than to peek at your phone when they are speaking to you.

If you want a culture of trust and openness, then give people your attention by putting down your phone when they walk in your office. Set the example. Prove to them that they are more important than information and watch your relationships grow.

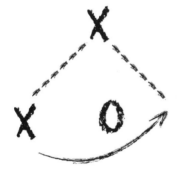

How will you put people first today?

My child, pay attention to what I say. Listen carefully to my words.

—*Proverbs 4:20*

success

Strive not to be a success,
but rather to be of value.

—Albert Einstein

You probably crafted some goals for your season, **BusyCoach**. Perhaps your team outlined what you're shooting for in terms of wins and team GPA. And maybe you even wrote down some personal goals you're working toward.

Success in sports is most often defined in wins, graduation rates and the like, and it's normal to strive for more in those areas. But Einstein offers a paradigm shift—challenging us to think in terms of adding value, instead of success.

Adding value describes how you show up—the attitude, effort and skills you bring to bear for the benefit of the team. You add value by bringing your best self to your team each day. By believing your presence matters.

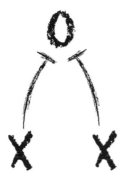

How will you add value today?

In his grace, God has given us different gifts for doing certain things well.

—Romans 12:6

motivation

 Moving people begins when you understand them, not when they understand you.

—Dan Rockwell

BusyCoaches are all about moving people—getting others to do what they don't want to do in order to achieve what they want to achieve. A pretty tall order, and even harder when you don't understand the people you're leading.

Learning about others' joys, defeats, motivations and temperaments gives you clues as to why they do what they do. Humans tend to make up stuff about one another, and often those assumptions are inaccurate.

Taking the time to get to know your teammates helps reduce off-base assumptions. Take them to lunch. Use quick getting-to-know-you exercises at the beginning of meetings. Utilize a temperament assessment as a discussion starter. Be curious about their lives.

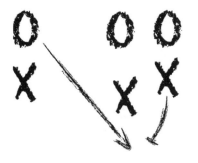

Remember, understanding your players will make motivating them easier.

For the LORD grants wisdom! From his mouth come knowledge and understanding.

—Proverbs 2:6

toughness

Toughness is in the soul and the spirit, not in the muscles.

—Alex Karras

Most of the factors that make a person tough exist on the inside, not the outside, **BusyCoach**.

Certainly one's physical presence and strength help, but you know plenty of athletes with lots of brawn who lack toughness. Players who fold under pressure or when adversity strikes.

Athletes who demonstrate unwavering toughness in critical moments display an inner strength that surpasses the external challenge.

Teach your players how to become tougher by investing time in developing their mental approach, self-talk or spiritual life, and they'll learn skills to help them overcome adversity in both sports and life.

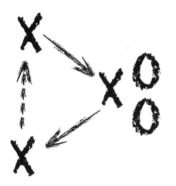

What will you do today to cultivate inner toughness in your players?

I pray that from his glorious, unlimited resources he will empower you with inner strength through his Spirit.

—Ephesians 3:16

humility

 People aren't attracted by what they see in you, but by what you see in them.

—Don Meyer

Many of us get easily caught up in how others perceive us, **BusyCoach**. It comes as naturally as the word "mine!" rolling off our tongues when we were young.

We may think that athletes, parents, fans or boosters are attracted to our leadership, team and program because of what they see in us—our charisma, intelligence or quick wit. Those are attractive qualities, but there's an even stronger magnet. The ability (and humility) to turn the spotlight on them.

When you tell someone what you see in them—their strengths, gifts, potential—it bolsters them. Even a constructive critique can draw people in. Affirmation gives people courage to be themselves and establishes a deeper connection between the recipient and the giver.

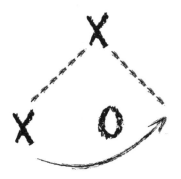

Share with someone what you see in them today and watch what happens!

So encourage each other and build each other up, just as you are already doing.

—1 Thessalonians 5:11

contentment

Learn how to be happy with what you have while you pursue all that you want.

—Jim Rohn

Contentment is learned, **BusyCoach**. It doesn't come naturally. In fact, discontentment is sometimes the fuel that drives people to do and be more. But it doesn't have to be that way.

It's possible to be content with your current status while pursuing something more. Not necessarily satisfied, but content.

Cultivating a thankful spirit for where you are today—the players on your roster, the staff with whom you lock arms, the money you have in your budget—fends off the dissatisfaction that comes from complaining and comparing.

Stay determined in pursuit of what you want, but do so with a light heart that finds happiness in the process of getting there and gratitude for what you have along the way.

In what ways are you learning contentment?

I have learned the secret of being content in any and every situation, whether well fed or hungry, whether living in plenty or in want. I can do all this through him who gives me strength.

—Philippians 4:12-13 (NIV)

confidence

 The quickest way to acquire
self-confidence is to do exactly
what you are afraid to do.

—Anon

There's a crisis of confidence among student-athletes, **BusyCoach**. Many garnered accolades from a young age for their athletic prowess. This, coupled with hovering parents protecting them from the uncomfortable, hard or unfair, has resulted in a myriad of young people whose confidence is shaken at the slightest bit of adversity.

As coaches and educators, you're positioned to show them how to fight through their fears. When you move toward your own fears (not around them), you inspire others to do the same. When you keep a big picture perspective (failure isn't fatal or final), you help your players grasp a growth mindset.

When your players are afraid to try a new skill in competition or hold a teammate accountable, encourage them to move toward it. Each time they do, what they fear will lose power over them. If they keep at it, their confidence will grow.

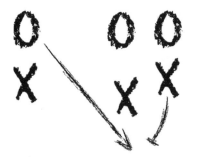 How will you inspire confidence in your athletes today?

But blessed is the one who trusts in the LORD, whose confidence is in him.

—*Jeremiah 17:7*

complacency

 Even if you're on the right track, you'll get run over if you just sit there.

—Will Rogers

Your team is moving in the right direction, **BusyCoach**. You created a team vision and goals, and everyone has bought in to where you're headed. Players and staff not only know, but embrace their roles.

Achieving goals requires the daily repetition over time of the right actions and habits. Every day seeking to get just 1 percent better. There's no such thing as an overnight success!

On the heels of reaching your goal, however, comes the threat of complacency—the temptation to sit still. The great ones keep moving, continually refining and improving their craft.

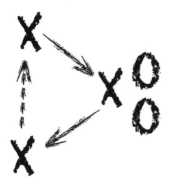

Resist complacency and keep moving!

But one thing I do: Forgetting what is behind and straining toward what is ahead, I press on toward the goal to win the prize for which God has called me heavenward in Christ Jesus.

—Philippians 3:13b-14 (NIV)

purpose

 If you live each day as if it
will be your last, one day you will
most certainly be right.

—Steve Jobs

Life comes with no guarantees, **BusyCoach**. No promise that you'll surpass the average life expectancy. No certainty that if you work your hardest you'll win a championship. No assurance that you'll avoid cancer.

There is just one sure thing: You and I will have a last day.

Steve Jobs asked himself everyday, "Would I want to engage in the work I face today if this was my last day?"

This question helped him stay on a path to spectacular innovations that not only lit his fire, but also transformed the way the world works, communicates and listens to music.

You only get one shot at your short time on this planet. Find what you love and do it. Make each day count.

Teach us to number our days, that we may gain a heart of wisdom.

—Psalm 90:12 (NIV)

waiting

Life is lived in the waiting.
—Jonathan Lockwood Huie

In a world that thrives on immediate gratification, we still spend lots of time waiting, **BusyCoach**. In fact, estimates reveal that Americans spend 37 billion hours per year waiting in lines.

We also wait in a larger sense: for the right next level job, for reconciliation in an important relationship, for the blue chip recruit to make up her mind. Waiting elicits feelings of frustration and anxiety. We want the direction, outcome or answer NOW.

The folks who keep leading, serving and loving during the wait make the best waiters. Rather than let discouragement paralyze them, they stay active during the wait.

No matter what you're waiting for, remember to live life in the waiting!

Then Abraham waited patiently, and he received what God had promised.

—Hebrews 6:15

INDEX